The Library of Explorers and Exploration

# HERNÁN CORTÉS

## The Conquest of Mexico and the Aztec Empire

Fred Ramen

the rosen publishing group's
rosen
central

*For Allison*

Published in 2004 by The Rosen Publishing Group, Inc.
29 East 21st Street, New York, NY 10010

**Library of Congress Cataloging-in-Publication Data**

Ramen, Fred.
Hernán Cortés : the Conquest of Mexico and the Aztec Empire /
Fred Ramen.— 1st ed.
    p. cm. — (The library of explorers and exploration)
Includes bibliographical references and index.
ISBN 0-8239-3622-8 (library binding )
1. Hernán Cortés, 1485–1547—Juvenile literature.
2. Mexico—History—Conquest, 1519–1540—Juvenile literature.
3. Mexico—Discovery and exploration—Spanish—Juvenile literature.
4. Conquerors—Mexico—Biography—Juvenile literature.
5. Explorers—Mexico—Biography—Juvenile literature.
6. Explorers—Spain—Biography—Juvenile literature.
I. Title. II. Series.
F1230.C35 R36 2003
972'.02'092—dc21

                                                2002004902

*Manufactured in the United States of America*

# ONTENTS

**FERDINANDO CORTES**
CAVATO DA VN ORIGINALE FATTO INAZI
CH'EI SI PORTASSI ALLA CONQVISTA DEL MESSICO.

# INTRODUCTION

## POWER AND CONQUEST

Although it is rare when a single person alters the course of history, as with the events surrounding rulers such as Alexander the Great or Napoleon Bonaparte, this is also the case with Spanish conquistador Hernán Cortés. His conquest of the ancient Aztec Empire and the rich lands of what is now present-day Mexico affected the entire world as much as Columbus's first trip across the Atlantic Ocean did.

In all of history, few events have affected the world as much as the discovery and subsequent conquest of the Americas. Besides the obvious changes that were brought about after 1492, such as the mingling of Indian and European cultures, the merging of once distant peoples brought about a new era of slavery, disease, and genocide. Other

Cortés and his small army, along with the help of thousands of Indian allies, were able to conquer the vast Aztec Empire. Cortés's success was the result of a combination of factors: the hatred of the Indian tribes for their Aztec over-lords; the belief that Cortés was a returning god; Cortés's qualities of leader-ship and diplomacy; superior European armaments; epidemics of diseases brought by Europeans; and the aid of Cortés's interpreter, Malinche.

changes were more subtle, but no less important, such as the introduction of florae and fauna from North America to Europe, as well as the introduction of new foods, such as tomatoes, corn, and chocolate, to the once bland European diet.

Because Spain had been largely responsible for this burst of worldwide exploration, its leaders would probably have inevitably instigated a conflict with the natives of the Americas during the sixteenth century. But under Cortés's dynamic leadership, the conquest took place with more speed and simplicity than Spain had thought possible. Cortés was a gambler who took risks, and with those risks he gained enormous ground. His boastful nature helped him forge a path few men could follow.

Cortés was a fascinating man, at once a mix of compassion and ruthlessness. He was also a devout Christian and a devious strategic mastermind who rose from obscurity in one of the poorest Spanish provinces to become one of its most important conquistadors. In doing so, he forged the destinies not only of two empires, but of two continents.

# 1

# BRAVE NEW WORLD

*He was a source of trouble to his parents as well as to himself, for he was restless, haughty, mischievous, and given to quarreling, for which reason he decided to seek his fortune.*
—Francisco López de Gómara, *History of the Conquest of Mexico*

During the eighth century, the Islamic Moors (Muslims) from North Africa conquered the Spanish Empire. At this unsettled time in the Mediterranean world, the new religion of Islam swept out of Arabia to conquer North Africa, Persia, sections of India, and later, Greece and areas now known as Turkey. Even facing such obstacles as crossing over the Pyrenees Mountains from Spain into France, the Moors nevertheless maintained control of parts of Europe, including Spain, for more than 700 years.

The response to this invasion was a long series of wars known in Spanish as the *Reconquista*, or the Reconquest. Gradually whittling away at the Moorish regions of Spain, the Christian kingdoms slowly expanded back across the Iberian Peninsula. In

this religious clash between Christianity and Islam, tensions were high on both sides. For the Spanish, the Reconquest became more than a patriotic struggle against an invader; it became a holy war, ordered by God. The Spanish wanted to drive all the infidels (nonbelievers) out of Spain in God's name.

The Muslims who were conquered by the Spanish were often made to suffer and were forced, sometimes violently, to convert to Christianity. The intolerance of the Spanish toward the Moors was extended to other non-Christian peoples, especially the Jews, who had found a refuge in Moorish Spain and had helped to make that region one of the most enlightened sections in all of Europe. This intolerance of other religions became an important characteristic of Spanish explorers' attitudes toward the native peoples they would meet throughout the New World.

## The New World

In 1492, the last Moorish region in Spain was finally reconquered. That same year, a Genoese

This image illustrates the Moors' surrender of Granada to Roman Catholic monarchs Ferdinand II and Isabella I in January 1492. As the seat of the Moorish kingdom, Granada was the final stronghold of the Moors in Spain. It is home to the Alhambra, a famed Moorish citadel and royal palace.

navigator sailed from Palos, Spain, with the support of the Spanish Crown. This man, Christopher Columbus, believed that the world was much smaller than his contemporaries thought. Therefore, he also firmly believed that reaching the East Indies could be accomplished more quickly by sailing west from Europe rather than around the tip of Africa, as the Portuguese believed. Although he was wrong about reaching the East Indies, he did find lands that would one day make Spain the richest kingdom in Europe.

Columbus, despite the fact that he truly believed he had reached the islands that bordered the coast of Asia, had not "discovered" the Americas either; they were already inhabited by millions of Native Americans when he began exploring the Caribbean Islands.

The Central and South American empires were remarkably sophisticated, especially when one considers that there were no animals such as horses available in the Americas. Moreover, before the Europeans arrived, the Mayan, Incan, and Aztec cultures had not grasped the importance of the wheel as a tool. But in the coming clash of civilizations, the accomplishments of cultures hundreds of years old were to be swept away by the guns, horses, and steel of the Spanish.

Into this world of rapid change and conflict was born Hernán Cortés. (His

This stone marker commemorates the birthplace of Hernán Cortés in Medellín, Spain. Except for the statue of his coat of arms, the village is much the same as it was during Cortés's early life.

name is often spelled Hernando, Fernan, or even Fernando, which are all more or less the same in Spanish; his last name is sometimes given as Cortez.) He was born in 1485, in the town of Medellín in Extremadura, one of the poorest sections of Spain, where his father, Martín Cortés, was a poor landowner. However, Martín was able to claim the title of *hidalgo*, or gentleman. Although not a noble, like a count or duke, he was above the common people even if he was poor. Unlike nobles, Martín Cortés had only pride to give to his son.

This seventeenth-century painting by Giovanni Manozzi illustrates the landing of the first Spaniards in America. Historians think the first Europeans who came to the Americas had very different visions from later settlers. The Spanish saw an opportunity to gain vast wealth: They were looking for gold and silver, valuable commodities that they could put on the ships and take back to Spain. The Spanish were also the first Europeans to establish a permanent presence in the Americas.

# A Young Man of Letters

Because he was very sickly, Hernán Cortés was not expected to survive past childhood. Last rites, or final prayers of absolution in the Christian religion, were said over the boy several times. In time, though, he grew to be a strong young man and an excellent horseman and swordfighter. He also developed his mind.

When he was fourteen years of age (or so he would later claim), he was sent by his parents to attend Salamanca, the greatest university in Spain, to become a lawyer. Whether or not he actually went, Cortés never earned a degree. (Some historians have speculated that he merely served as a clerk to a lawyer.) But it is known that he could read and write, and not only Spanish, but Latin. He also had at least a basic grasp of the complex Spanish legal system. As we will see, this knowledge of the law would later serve him well during his conquest of Mexico.

For whatever reason, Cortés returned home from school after only two years. The sixteen-year-old boy was now a rebellious young man. Because of his unruly attitude his parents decided that it would be best if he left their house and found his own way in the world.

# Choosing His Path

At this point, during the early sixteenth century, there were two paths that a young Spaniard might choose. One was to go to Italy and join the Spanish war against the French being waged there. The other was to follow Columbus's path to the New World and the tiny Spanish colonies in the Caribbean Islands. Although the islands had proved to be disappointing in some ways—they were certainly not the Molucca Islands (Spice Islands) of the East Indies that were the original goal of Columbus—they did offer tantalizing hints of wealth to come, especially in gold. The Spanish adventurers, known as conquistadors, often returned from the New World to Spain wearing golden ornaments, a sign of what future exploration of the region might bring. The choice was easy for Cortés. He would travel to the New World in search of riches and new lands.

In the end, however, his voyage was put on hold. The cause of his delay was a woman, for the young Cortés had become a notorious womanizer and had had many affairs. One night, while walking along the top of a wall returning from meeting a married woman, the wall crumbled beneath his feet and he fell into a garden. He nonetheless was badly injured and soon fell ill. The fleet his parents had arranged for him to sail with to the New World departed without him.

This fifteenth-century woodcut shows a Spanish ship sailing near Hispaniola and its surrounding islands. This image was published with a letter to King Ferdinand and Queen Isabella from Columbus detailing his discoveries in the New World.

When he had recovered from his injuries and illness, Cortés decided he would go to Italy instead of the West Indies, and his parents raised the money for this trip as well. But again, he did not go. Instead, Cortés wandered around Spain, often penniless and hungry. Without direction in his life, his original idea of traveling to the New World in search of easy money must have begun to look better. Eventually, he returned to Medellín and begged his parents once more for the money to sail to the New World. Perhaps glad to finally be rid of their rebellious son, they were able to

Atlantic

Windward Passage

Île de la Tortue

Port-de-Paix

Cap-Haïtien

Gonaïves

Golfe de
la Gonâve

St. Marc

Hinche

**HAITI**

Île de
la Gonâve

Jérémie

PORT-AU-PRINCE

Lago

MESSIF DE LA

Pétionville

MASSIF DE LA SELLE

Les Cayes

Jacmel

Isla Beata

Hispaniola is the second largest island of the West
Indies. It is now divided into the republic of Haiti
(west) and the Dominican Republic (east). The island's
area is 29,530 sq. miles (76,483 sq. km). Columbus
landed on the island in 1492 and named it La Isla
Española, which was later Anglicized to Hispaniola.
   During Spanish colonial times Hispaniola was
commonly called Santo Domingo (Saint Dominic in
English). The island's position on the northern flank of
the Caribbean Sea provided an excellent location for
the Spanish to expand into Cuba, Mexico, Panama,
and South America during the early colonial period.

Caribbean Se

72°

*an*

# HISPANIOLA

20° N

Puerto Plata

antiago    San Francisco
           de Macorís

    La Vega
▲10,128 ft

A CENTRAL    **DOMINICAN**

              **REPUBLIC**

Azua    San Cristóbel

arahona         SANTO      La Romana
                DOMINGO

18° N

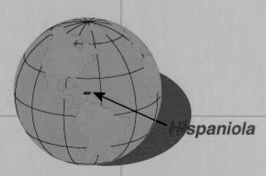

Hispaniola

70° W                                    68° W

gather enough money to send Cortés across the ocean to Hispaniola, the main Spanish colony in the West Indies.

## Hispaniola

Cortés's sea voyage was a miserable one. The captain of his ship tried to beat the rest of the fleet across the ocean, only to get completely lost. Nearly starving and almost out of water, the ship's crew finally sighted a white dove, a bird that could only have come from land, on Good Friday in the year 1504. Two days later, on Easter Sunday, Cortés landed in the New World.

At nineteen years of age, Cortés arrived in Santo Domingo, the town founded by Columbus in Hispaniola and the center of the Spanish Empire in the West Indies. He was poor, but in Hispaniola even a poor man could live like a lord—or so it seemed.

Cortés was granted a small parcel of land and Indian slaves to farm it. He was told that if he stayed with his land for five years he would own it. This was the infamous Spanish practice called the *encomienda*, designed as an alternative to outright slavery. The Spanish lord of the land parcel was expected to provide for the welfare of the Indians and educate them in Christianity. This system was little better and often worse than slavery, as the Spanish often cruelly mistreated the Native Americans.

European explorers and settlers were often very cruel to the native peoples of the New World. They sometimes justified their acts of violence by claiming that they were on a mission to educate them in matters of religion—Catholicism—and civility. Still, some of the Indians' greatest advocates were, in fact, Catholic clergymen. Both the Catholic Church and the Spanish Crown attempted to institute regulations to protect the Indians against slavery and mistreatment, often with little influence against conquistador landowners who wanted absolute authority over them. These acts of violence, often unprovoked, changed forever the lives of the original Americans.

At the time, Cortés had no intention of staying anywhere in the New World for as long as five years, as he told the clerk who assigned him his land. But he was, in fact, fated to stay there for seven long years, an obscure colonist with nothing to mark him as exceptional.

He remained a wild, impulsive, and sometimes even violent, young man. He had frequent affairs with the Indian women of the island, and entered into at least one duel, a sword fight that left him scarred on his chin; it was a mark he later covered with a beard. At the same time, Cortés found more respectable work acting as a notary public (a public position requiring some knowledge of the law) in the village of Azúa, about fifty miles from Santo Domingo.

## Future Dreams

Toward the end of this period, Cortés is said to have had an unusual dream in which he was surrounded by strange people who addressed him with great reverence. He was wearing rich garments and was in an obvious position of honor and respect. When he told other people about his dream, it seemed like a prophecy of things to come.

In 1511, the twenty-six-year-old Cortés made his first move to establish a name for himself in the New World. An expedition was being organized to conquer the nearby island of Cuba, and Cortés served as a secretary to its commander, Diego Velázquez.

Velázquez was one of the original settlers of Santo Domingo and a veteran of Spain's many wars. He had become one of the most important men in Hispaniola, founding several towns. A heavyset man with mild manners, Velázquez was also a devious politician and ruthless commander.

Velázquez had ordered the massacre of many of the peaceful Indians of Hispaniola, and he did likewise in Cuba, where there was little resistance to the Spanish invasion. He also tried to use the expedition to grab more land and glory for himself. Cortés, who became close to Velázquez, observed his behavior firsthand, and may have learned many lessons from the older, more experienced man.

Meanwhile, almost by chance, events were set in place that would shake both Europe and the Americas. Cortés would find trouble and fortune in Cuba, and a rivalry with his former commander that would nearly lead to his death. Yet this same commander would conclude that Cortés was precisely the man he needed to undertake the riskiest adventure ever attempted in the New World. In this Velázquez was right, but not in the manner for which he may have hoped.

# 2

# INTO THE UNKNOWN

*Valor loves not idleness, and so, therefore, if you will take hope for valor, or valor for hope, and if you do not abandon me, as I shall not abandon you, I shall make you in a very short time the richest of all men who have crossed the seas, and of all the armies that have here made war. You are few, I see, but such is your spirit that no effort or force of Indians will prevail against you.*

—Hernán Cortés

The Spanish conquest of Mexico was greatly influenced by specific human relationships of the time. Had Cortés not befriended Velázquez during his expedition to Cuba, it is unlikely that he would ever have had the chance to go to Mexico. But during the years before the Cuban governor selected him to lead an expedition to the North American mainland, the two had become bitter rivals. This rivalry would resurface during Cortés's time in America and nearly destroy everything he had accomplished, eventually leading to the deaths of many Spaniards and countless Native Americans.

Diego Velázquez, governor of Cuba, laid the foundation for the Spanish conquest of Mexico. In 1517 and 1518 Velázquez sent out expeditions to explore the coasts of the Yucatán Peninsula and the Gulf of Mexico. Velázquez then commissioned Cortés to investigate tales of great wealth in the area. Spending his own fortune and a portion of Velázquez's, Cortés left Havana in November 1518.

Understanding the conflict between Cortés and Velázquez is crucial to understanding much of what happened later. It may well have driven Cortés to take many of the risks he took in America. Yet Velázquez's choice of Cortés is a mysterious one: It is unknown why he would choose a man he had struggled against for years to command such a vital mission of exploration.

# The Xuárez Family

The origin of the feud lay in the two men's relations with the Xuárez family. The family, consisting of Juan Xuárez, his sister, whose name was unrecorded, and her two daughters, Catalina and Leonor, had immigrated to the West Indies from Spain in 1509. The two girls were ladies-in-waiting to Doña Maria de Cuellar, herself a lady-in-waiting to Maria de Toledo, wife of Diego Columbus, Christopher Columbus's son who was the viceroy of the Indies. Diego Velázquez became engaged to Maria de Cuellar while she lived in Santo Domingo; after he conquered Cuba, she moved there to marry him. The Xuárez family accompanied her to the new colony.

Catalina Xuárez was very beautiful, and she caught the eye of Cortés, who, at the time, was a successful businessman in Cuba. His service to Velázquez had been rewarded with one of the best estates on the island; gold had been discovered on his land, and Cortés was beginning to build a fortune. Soon Cortés started a relationship with Catalina. Meanwhile, Maria de Cuellar had died not long after marrying Velázquez, and afterward he became involved with Catalina's sister, Leonor.

Historians are uncertain about how these events unfolded, however. They believe that Cortés's relationship with Catalina had become more serious, prompting the young woman to expect a marriage proposal from her suitor. For reasons that are unknown, Cortés refused to propose—a shocking breach of courtesy for the day—which made Velázquez dislike him for shaming the family of the woman with whom he was romantically linked. Then, to worsen matters, Cortés openly made himself an enemy of the powerful Cuban governor.

As was his right as the commander of the expedition that had conquered the island, Velázquez had handed out estates to the Spanish soldiers who had accompanied him based on his personal whim. Cortés, who had done well for himself, had no complaints about these actions, as other men did. They wanted to appeal the division of land to a panel of judges recently sent to Hispaniola to oversee the Spanish colonies. They wrote letters and acquired documents that they felt proved that Velázquez had been unfair. Specifically, they felt that the land given to the Spaniards had been distributed unevenly. But these disgruntled men needed an educated man of influence to plead their case to the judges in Santo Domingo. Their obvious choice for spokesman was unanimous: They wanted Cortés to represent their argument before the judge.

## Cortés as a Diplomat

It is unclear why Cortés would have wanted to accept this assignment. He had not suffered from Velázquez's division of land. In fact, his close relationship to the governor had turned out quite well for him. Yet he chose to risk not only his position, but also his life. The plan, which called for a hazardous trip to Santo Domingo in a canoe, was a dangerous one, for Cortés had to face the political enemies of the most powerful man in Cuba.

Unfortunately, we can only speculate on Cortés's motivations. Perhaps he really felt that Velázquez had treated the other Spaniards unfairly, and wanted to bring them justice. This is a strong possibility, mainly because Cortés was known for speaking critically about the encomienda system while in Hispaniola. Perhaps he wanted to distinguish himself by arguing an important legal case before the judges in Santo Domingo. Or, perhaps he interpreted the unrest of the other Spaniards as a sign that Velázquez's power in Cuba was weakening. This may be the most likely explanation, for Cortés had an uncanny instinct for knowing when a person's position had weakened, and when to move against him.

In colonial days, punishment was very harsh, as seen in this nineteenth-century print by George H. Walker. Different methods of punishment included using devices such as the stocks or pillory *(above)*, or the whipping post, or branding and maiming an offender's body. The stocks were a frame of timber with holes used to confine the feet or hands (or both) of offenders. This was mainly for embarrassment, but people were often left trapped for days.

However, in this particular case, Cortés's cunning instincts were wrong. Velázquez somehow found out what Cortés was planning and had him arrested. The two men, once companions and friends, were now bitter enemies. To make matters worse for Cortés, Catalina was suing him for breach of contract—for failing to marry her after promising that he would. Still acting as the governor of Cuba, Velázquez ordered Cortés placed in the stocks, where he would have been publicly ridiculed. But the wily Cortés was not yet beaten.

27

# Escape

Somehow Cortés escaped from the stocks, either by prying open the lock or bribing his guards. Fleeing Velázquez's men, he took refuge in a church and asked for sanctuary. This was a time-honored tradition that meant as long as Cortés stayed in the church, he could not be arrested or harmed. However, he was soon lured out of the building—perhaps by Catalina, who had come to speak with him—and arrested by soldiers led by a man named Juan Escudero. (Years later, during the conquest of Mexico, Cortés had Escudero hanged, surely seeking revenge for having been captured by him in Cuba.)

This time Cortés was chained and thrown into the hold of a ship that was to sail to Hispaniola, where he would be tried by the very judges he had hoped to appear in front of to attack Velázquez. Once again, however, he managed to escape— almost certainly by bribery—and stole a small boat. Unable to fight the current, he swam back to Cuba, with the documents that he hoped would condemn Velázquez wrapped in a handkerchief tied to his head to keep them dry.

Again he took sanctuary in a church, but this time he made sure to improve his position before he left. Juan Xuárez and he resolved their differences; Cortés agreed to marry Catalina, and Xuárez agreed to drop the lawsuit.

Cortés then managed to reconcile with Velázquez, too, for the moment ending their feud. Velázquez even became the godfather of a child Cortés had fathered with an Indian woman.

## A Bid for Greater Power

In 1513, Cortés was engaged to Catalina, and although he waited for two years to actually marry her, they lived together as if they were already husband and wife. He had been in the New World for nearly a decade and was making his fortune. In the years to come, he twice served as *alcalde*, or mayor, of Santiago, one of the largest towns in Cuba. The headstrong, restless years of his youth were over. Although he would remain an impulsive man, and one who would take risks until the end of his life, he now showed that he possessed patience.

Unlike many of the other Spaniards, Cortés carefully worked his estate using superior planting techniques. He conserved the gold found on his land, trying to discover the richest veins rather than just grabbing what was easiest to obtain. Cortés also became friendly with other landowners throughout Cuba, and gained a reputation as a gracious and generous host. Although he may not have known it at the time, Cortés was laying the groundwork for his eventual successes in Mexico.

This detail of a fresco painting by Diego Rivera depicts the arrival of Cortés at Vera Cruz. Using his charm and cunning wiles, as well as his money, Cortés went from imprisonment in the stocks to being one of the wealthiest men in Cuba in just a few years.

The soldier of fortune Bernal Díaz del Castillo, who would later serve with Cortés in Mexico as well as write one of the most important histories of the conquest, first met Cortés around this time. His description of Cortés was a flattering one. Besides commenting on his strong stature, Castillo wrote that Cortés had a "somewhat pale complexion and serious expression. If his features lacked something it was because they were too small, his eyes mild and grave. His beard and hair were black and thin . . . His legs were bowed and he was an excellent horseman . . . when he was angry the veins in his throat and forehead would stand out, and when he was very angry he would not talk at all."

Cortés seemed to have fulfilled all of his dreams. Besides owning a rich estate in the New World, he was in a position of power and respect. He was married to a beautiful woman with connections to the rulers of the Spanish New World. Then, in 1517, events occurred that would bring him even greater power, riches, and fame.

## Mysterious Lands

Strangely enough, twenty-five years after Columbus's first trip to the West Indies, the Spanish had still not explored much to the west of Cuba and Hispaniola. Although there were rumors of a land that might be a large island in that direction, no one had ventured to explore it. Needing more Indian slaves to work the plantations and mines of Cuba, Velázquez authorized an expedition of three ships and more than a hundred men (including Bernal Díaz del Castillo) under the command of Francisco Hernández de Córdoba to explore present-day Central America and capture Indian slaves.

They returned much worse for their wear. They had discovered several developments made of stone on the Yucatán (a large peninsula that juts out from the coast of what is now southern Mexico), the first actual cities that the

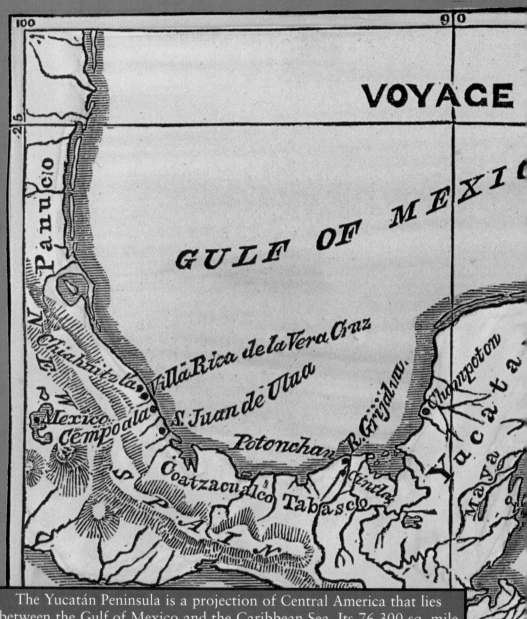

The Yucatán Peninsula is a projection of Central America that lies between the Gulf of Mexico and the Caribbean Sea. Its 76,300 sq. mile (197,600 sq. km) territory includes the modern Mexican states of Campeche, Quintana Roo, and Yucatán, and parts of Belize and Guatemala. Cortés signed an agreement appointing him captain general of the expedition to the Yucatán Peninsula in October 1518. His experience of the rough-and-tumble New World politics forced Cortés to hastily plan his trip before Velázquez changed his mind.

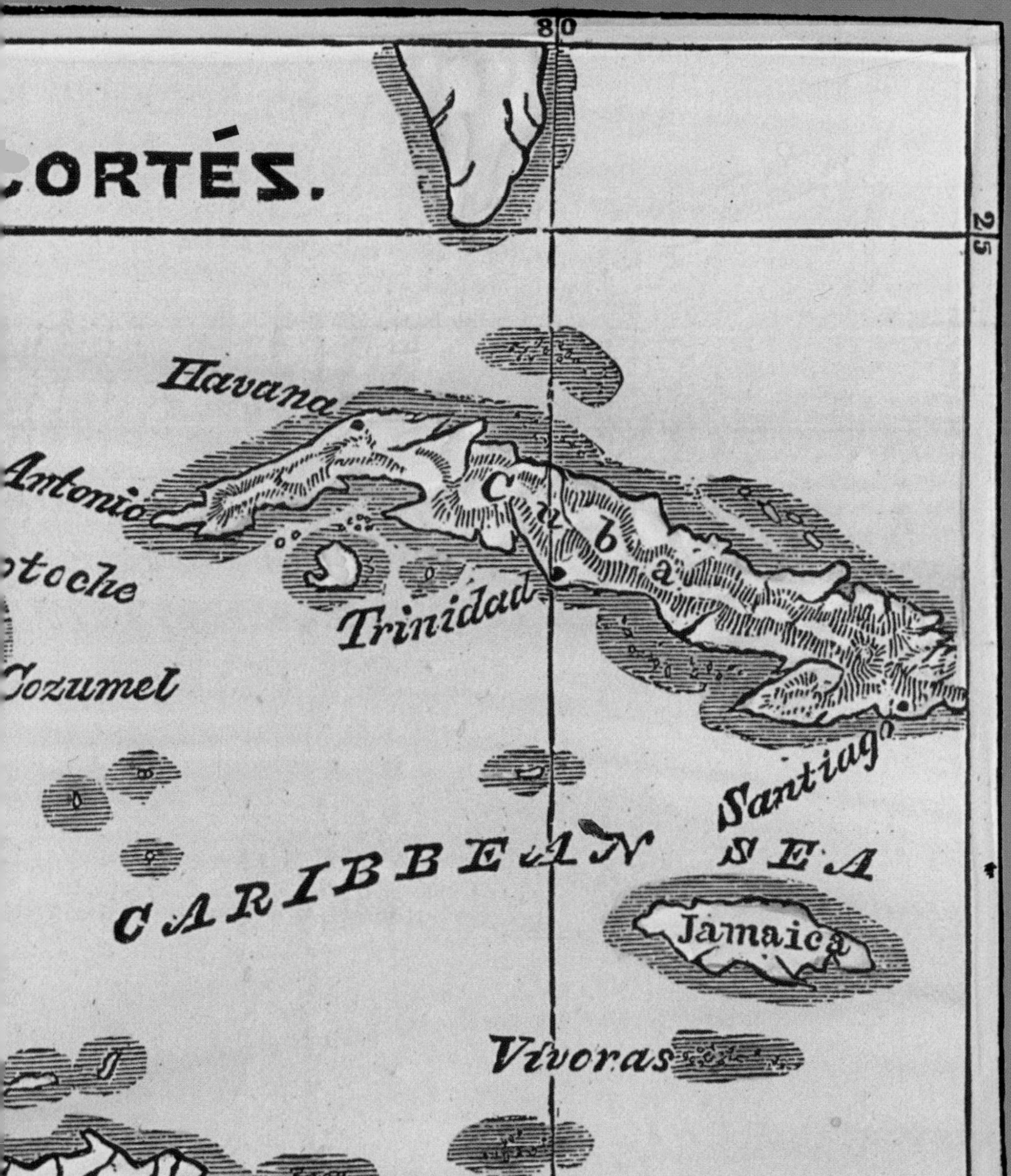
CORTÉS.
80
25
Havana
Antonio
otoche
C u b a
Trinidad
Cozumel
Santiago
CARIBBEAN SEA
Jamaica
Vivoras
ras
C. Gracias á Dios
15
80

In 1518 Velázquez sent out Juan de Grijalva *(above)* to explore the coasts of the Yucatán Peninsula and the Gulf of Mexico. On this trip de Grijalva came upon Cozumel, which Cortés later explored.

Spanish had seen in the New World. But the native inhabitants had attacked them. They had escaped with a small amount of gold taken from a native couple, Mayan Indians whom the Spanish named Juan and Melchior.

Velázquez was interested in what Córdoba had found. The gold the Spanish had discovered in Hispaniola and Cuba had never amounted to much; the "island" of Yucatán, so much larger than either Cuba or Hispaniola, promised to have much more of the precious metal. He authorized another expedition, this one under his nephew, Juan de Grijalva. While Grijalva was gone, Velázquez, worrying that his nephew might try to claim the land for himself, sent another expedition out under the command of Cristóbal de Olid. When Olid's ship was late in returning, he began to plan yet another expedition, this one led by Cortés. It marked the first time that Cortés ever showed an interest in the newly discovered lands to the west.

# The First Expedition

That Velázquez chose Cortés to lead the expedition after so much bad blood had passed between them seems unusual. Indeed, Cortés was not his first choice. But his favorite lieutenants were either in Spain or unwilling to put up the money that Velázquez demanded as their share of the expenses for the voyage. Around this same time, Cortés secretly met with two high-placed advisers to Velázquez and made a deal with them: If they would support him for the leadership of the expedition, he would split his share of the profits.

By now, one of the ships of Grijalva's fleet had returned to Cuba laden with gold. Soon the remaining ships of Grijalva's and Olid's fleets returned, too. Grijalva told of finding an island named Cozumel, and of a region called Tabasco, after a native chief by the same name, where they were welcomed. To the north and west of Tabasco they had come across richly dressed Indians who had given them gold and jewels. These tales, and others like them, increased interest in the new expedition.

Velázquez gave Cortés a number of instructions. He was to treat the native people well and teach them about Christianity, as well as about the king of Spain. The explorers were instructed not to take anything from the Indians by force. He was also required to search for any shipwrecked Spaniards who might be in the area.

Velázquez told Cortés not to venture inland, but to instead sleep each night on the ship. He was to take possession of all the lands he found for Spain, but no mention was made of establishing any settlements. Velázquez clearly wanted to settle the lands, because then he would be able to claim all the territory he found for himself, not the viceroy of the Indies, who was his superior and legally entitled to anything found by Velázquez's expeditions.

Cortés readily agreed to all of these conditions, and quickly set about preparing for the journey. He ordered a fine banner, embroidered with a Christian cross in gold thread and the message "Comrades, in true faith let us follow the Holy Cross and together we will conquer." He hired a crier to go through the towns of Cuba and proclaim that anyone who accompanied him would receive a share of treasure gained by the expedition, as well as a grant of land and Indians. More than 300 men decided to join him.

He also tended to practical matters. Cortés took supplies, such as food and oil; trade goods, such as glass beads, mirrors, and ribbons; weapons, especially crossbows, primitive firearms known as harquebuses, and several small cannons; and horses. Cortés spared no expense in gathering everything he thought he would need for the trip, including mortgaging his property and subsequently going into debt. This behavior caused Velázquez to become suspicious.

This painting depicts Cortés hurrying his ships out to sea from Santiago. He landed in Mexico and subsequently freed himself from Velázquez's overlordship by founding the city of Vera Cruz. Soon after, Cortés established a town council that empowered him to conquer Mexico in the name of King Charles I of Spain.

Whatever Cortés was planning, it seemed clear that it was not going to be limited only to trading with the natives of the new lands. Thinking that Velázquez would try to remove him from the expedition entirely, Cortés ordered his men to take all the meat they could from local storehouses, and then quickly put to sea from Santiago in November.

His fleet sailed along the coast of Cuba, stopping to pick up more men and supplies along the way. Velázquez tried to arrest

37

him twice, but Cortés, now coming into his own as a leader, was able to convince the governor's men not to take him in. His leadership abilities, most likely along with a few well-placed bribes, kept the expedition stable.

In February 1519, Cortés assembled his men on the western tip of Cuba. He had 11 ships, 16 horses, several large and small cannons, and more than 650 men, some outfitted with weapons such as swords, crossbows, and small field guns called falconers and harquebuses. His force probably comprised more than a thousand men; it was easily the largest expedition ever organized there. What Cortés planned to do with his team was unclear, perhaps even to him. But it was certain that he would not be content with merely trading on a small scale with the coastal cities. Cortés had planned for a greater glory, and had brought with him all the tools he needed to find it.

# 3

# EMPIRES OF THE SUN

*I spoke of a great lord called Mutezuma, whom the natives of these lands had spoken to me about . . . I decided to go and see him wherever he might be. Indeed, I remember that, with respect to the quest of this lord, I undertook more than I was able, for I assured Your Highness that I would take him alive in chains and make him subject to Your Majesty's Royal Crown.*

—Hernan Cortés, in a letter to Charles, king of Spain and Holy Roman Emperor

Cortés's destination as his fleet sailed from Cuba was the island of Cozumel, discovered by Juan de Grijalva's expedition of the previous year. The natives of the island were known to be more like those of Cuba and Hispaniola, and not likely to attack the Spaniards as had the fierce warriors of the mainland. The captain of one of Cortés's ships, Pedro de Alvarado, who had also been in Grijalva's expedition, disobeyed Cortés's orders and landed on Cozumel two days before the rest of the fleet. The men of that ship raided the villages of the natives, stealing food and some gold trinkets that they found in temples.

Not for the last time, Cortés, was furious with the redheaded Alvarado, a headstrong young man who perhaps reminded Cortés of himself. Alvarado returned the gold the Spaniards had stolen from the temples and paid for the food they had taken with metal tools and green-colored glass beads. The Indians, who mistook the glass for jade, prized the trinkets even more so than they did gold. Along with the help of a captured Mayan whom the Spanish named Melchior, Cortés destroyed their pagan idols and instead erected crosses and a shrine to the Catholic Virgin Mary. Cortés, having brought a supply of wooden images of the Virgin to give to the Indians he encountered, conquered and converted the entire island with little effort.

## Jerónimo de Aguilar

While in Cozumel, Grijalva's expedition had heard rumors of shipwrecked Spaniards who were living on the mainland. Cortés sent an Indian there in search of these men and, amazingly enough, he found one of them.

The island of Cozumel, an outpost of the ancient Maya from AD 800, served as a month-long respite for Cortés and his crew. Besides introducing Christian crosses to the natives of the island, Cortés and his men destroyed many of their shrines to Ixchel, the Mayan goddess of the moon, the sea, and fertility.

The Spaniard was a priest named Jerónimo de Aguilar, one of only two remaining survivors of a doomed voyage from Panama to Hispaniola that had been shipwrecked off of the Yucatán. The other survivor, Gonzal Guerrero, had married the daughter of a chief and become a famous warrior while Aguilar had become a slave. Using more green-colored glass beads that Cortés had sent with the courier, Aguilar bought his freedom from slavery and traveled to Cozumel.

The union of Aguilar and Cortés became very useful because Aguilar could speak both Mayan and Spanish well, and he took over as translator. He confirmed Cortés's suspicion that a land rich with gold lay to the west. In keeping with his plan to reach this land of gold, Cortés decided to travel next to the region of Tabasco, where Grijalva had heard about the region and its rumored treasures. When Grijalva had visited the area, the inhabitants had traded with him without being provoked. But Cortés found that their attitude had changed.

Sailing up the Tabasco River with about eighty of his men, Cortés found a settlement protected by a stockade, a high wall made of logs planted like posts in the ground. Using Aguilar to translate, Cortés told the inhabitants of the town that he only wanted to buy supplies of food and water. In fact, he needed neither; his request was actually a test to see if the Indians would obey him.

# The Attack at Tabasco

The Tabascans brought a large supply of food, but Cortés demanded more. Then he asked permission to enter the town and look for the food himself. They told Cortés that he must wait until the following day before beginning his own search for supplies. Clearly fearing an attack, the Tabascans sent the women and children out of town during the night.

They were right to fear it, for that was what Cortés had in store. He gathered his remaining men and sent several hundred of them across the river. His plan was to have them attack the town from behind.

The next day, the Tabascans brought Cortés more provisions. But because they had no more food to offer, the Tabascans demanded that Cortés leave. Cortés then ordered Aguilar to read the *requerimiento* to the Tabascans. This was a document that the conquistadors were legally bound to read to any of the native peoples they encountered before fighting with them. It was a brief explanation of the Christian faith and a message stating that, as God's representative on Earth, the pope had given all the lands in the New World to Spain and that all its inhabitants must show obedience to the king. If they did not, they would be considered rebels and dealt with harshly.

43

Spanish military dominance greatly helped Cortés in his conquest of Mexico and the surrounding lands. The Spanish had the cavalry, steel armor, and firepower to overwhelm the native peoples and used swords made of strong, hard steel. They also had armor that repelled Indian projectiles and weakened the blows from the natives' obsidian (volcanic glass) swords. Because their wounds were limited to the limbs, face, neck, and other unprotected regions, Spanish soldiers faced less risk of death, while the unarmored Indians were very vulnerable.

While most conquistadors never even bothered to read the requerimiento, Cortés, with his legal training, always made a point of having it read. The Tabascans, however, merely laughed and prepared for a conflict. Melchior, who had deserted Cortés, had told the Tabascans to fight well. He knew that the Tabascans had to crush the Spanish now while they had the ability.

The confrontation became Cortés's first major battle, and the first one in the conquest of Mexico. Although the Indians heavily outnumbered him, Cortés and his men had several advantages. One of the Spaniards' benefits was their weaponry of steel swords and spears. The Indians had only stone weapons, although one of these, a heavy club lined with razor-sharp bits of glassy stone called obsidian, could cause serious bodily damage. Another advantage that the Spaniards had was their crossbows and primitive muskets. While the muskets were not as reliable as the crossbows, the noise and smoke they produced often panicked the natives, as did the sight of their horses, never before seen in parts of the New World. (Although he had several small cannons, Cortés did not use them for this battle.)

The Spanish were also more disciplined soldiers who fought as a unit, instead of attacking in a mass of individuals as the Indians did. But their biggest advantage was their cavalry. The Indians, deathly afraid of the men on horseback, thought at first that animal and rider were all one creature, half-man and half-beast.

Cortés led his men from the river toward the town through a shower of arrows and stones shot by native defenders from behind the stockade. Soon Cortés's remaining men, hidden behind the town, joined the fight. It wasn't long before the Spanish were inside the town, with its defenders dead, wounded, or fleeing for their lives.

Cortés ordered a search of the area for gold and other valuables, but none were found. He dramatically cut three slashes into a sacred tree with his sword and claimed the country for Spain. Shortly afterward, Cortés established his own quarters inside the town's temple. Still, he knew that the conflict was far from finished. For several days, little happened. Patrols sent out from Tabasco had small fights with the Indians without major battles, although one fight escalated so much that Cortés was forced to use his cannon, the effects of which were devastating.

# A Spanish Victory

The following day, Cortés marched his entire force out onto a nearby plain. His plan was to confront the Tabascans, who had summoned their allies to fight with them, making their force a much stronger unit. Bernal Díaz del Castillo wrote in *The Conquest of New Spain* that they surrounded the Spaniards like "mad dogs," but were subdued, in

The Spanish military superiority over the native peoples enabled them to conquer the Tabascans with relative ease. The Spanish not only had better weapons and armor, but they also fought in a regimented fashion with many backup units, in contrast with the Tabascans, who engaged in individual hand-to-hand combat. In addition, the advantage of the sixteen horses the Spanish brought with them cannot be overstated. Spanish cavalry charges caused the frightened Indians to retreat in terror. According to Bernal Díaz de Castillo, "The Indians thought at the time that the horse and rider were one creature, for they had never seen a horse before." This engraving was copied from a painting made by Alonzo Chappel in 1870.

part, by cannon fire. His account continued, "Mesa, our artilleryman, killed many of them with his cannon, for they were formed in great squadrons and they did not open out, so that he could fire at them as he pleased, but with all the hurts and wounds we gave them we could not drive them off."

At this moment, Cortés and his cavalry attacked the Indians. Unable to outrun the men on horseback, many of the Tabascans died at the hands of the Spanish, who speared or slashed them with their steel swords. Not surprisingly, the Tabascans fled the battlefield in disorder and soon surrendered. They gave the Spanish small amounts of gold—all they had—and told them that they had only fought because their neighboring tribes had belittled them for not facing the Spanish a year earlier. The Tabascans also gave Cortés and his men gifts of food and female slaves, one of whom would later mean as much to Cortés as any of his strongest men.

Her name was Malinali Tenepal, a designation that referred not only to her date of birth in the Aztec calendar, but also to her horoscope. For, according to the Aztecs, Tenepal, also known as Malinche, was a woman destined to thrive in conflict, and who would speak much and with great liveliness. She was one of twenty female slaves given to the Spaniards, who renamed her Doña Marina. She was beautiful, and

Malinche became Cortés's mistress, guide, and interpreter; in fact, the success of his ventures is directly attributable to her linguistic abilities. Her knowledge of the Mayan and Nahuatl languages helped the Spaniards get out of many perilous situations and enabled them to conquer Mexico. Malinche served her adopted countrymen with dedication. She bore Cortés a son, Martín, and later married one of his soldiers, Juan de Jaramillo, with whom she went to Spain, where she was warmly received at the Spanish Court.

was said to be the daughter of a chief who had died young. Her mother had sold her into slavery because she had remarried another chief. After she was in the hands of the Spanish, Cortés gave Malinche to one of his favorite captains, Alonso Hernández de Puertocarrero.

Doña Marina, whom the Indians now called Malinche (the suffix *che* literally meant girl or woman), was the most important person Cortés would meet in Mexico. For Malinche not only spoke Mayan, the language Aguilar spoke, but she also spoke Nahuatl, the language of the Aztecs. At first Malinche translated Nahuatl into Mayan, and Aguilar would translate her Mayan words to Spanish. Soon, however, she spoke enough Spanish to speak directly to Cortés.

From the first day, Malinche served Cortés with total loyalty, as if she knew immediately that their destinies would be forever linked. Without her assistance, Cortés could not have easily spoken with the Aztecs. He would have been at the mercy of an empire of millions had he not been able to communicate clearly and effectively. Malinche was the key person responsible for his ability to understand the Aztec people, and with her help he was able to achieve one of the most improbable conquests in history. Because of her solid loyalty to Cortés, many contemporary Mexicans have forever remembered Malinche as a traitor. They consider her the woman who gave their country to a foreign invader.

# Cortés, the Leader

Cortés was now a proven leader. Having led his men in a winning battle and defeating a much larger force of Indians, he now decided to move closer to the mysterious land of Mexico, which he believed was the source of all the New World's golden wealth. On Good Friday 1519, he landed at a place Grijalva had called San Juan de Ulua. Once there, they were met by representatives of the Aztec Empire, of whom they had only heard rumors and who began supplying the Spaniards with food and other items. Unlike Grijalva, who had also met with Aztec ambassadors, Cortés could communicate with them with Malinche's help. He told them that he was a representative of Charles I, the new Spanish king who was also Emperor Charles V of the Holy Roman Empire, and that he had been sent on a mission to speak with the Aztec emperor, whose great empire was known to Charles. This was a lie, but Cortés was already forming his plan to reach the Aztec capital, Tenochtitlán, without having to fight.

After sending messengers to Tenochtitlán, the Aztecs brought Cortés presents of gold and silver, but told him that he could not meet with their emperor because he was too ill to make the journey. The trip to Tenochtitlán was also a dangerous one for the Spaniards. Cortés insisted and politely said that he could not leave the country until he had

King Charles I of Spain (1516 to 1556), who was also Holy Roman Emperor (1519 to 1556), struggled to hold his empire together against the growing forces of Protestantism, increasing pressure from the Turkish and the French, and even hostility from the pope.

met with the emperor; the long and dangerous trip would be nothing after a journey of thousands of miles. While hoping that the Spaniards would decide to leave, the Aztecs continued to offer them gifts of gold. However, in an effort to drive them away from their lands, the Aztecs soon stopped giving them food altogether.

Facing starvation, Cortés had another problem. A large group of his men argued that they should return to Cuba. They begged Cortés to leave San Juan de Ulua. Expressing that they already had an enormous treasure of gold, they reasoned that it made sense to leave before the entire expedition starved or faced certain death at the hands of the fierce Aztec warriors. Cortés, however, had no intention of leaving. He had already violated his orders by fighting with the Tabascans and certainly would be arrested if he returned to Cuba. Luckily, Cortés had an alternative solution.

Using the experience he had gained during his legal education, Cortés proposed that the Spaniards found a settlement on the mainland. Some of the men who still supported him quickly agreed to the idea and set up a town council, even though not a single building had been erected. Cortés then resigned as the head of Velázquez's expedition, and was appointed captain-general of the new town of Villa Rica de la Vera Cruz ("Rich Town of the True Cross"). Because new colonies came under the direct control of the king, Cortés got out of having to obey Velázquez's orders by using this tactic. In doing so, he would get a much larger share of anything the Spaniards gained in Mexico.

## "Conquer, or Die!"

In order to make sure that King Charles would support his attempted rebellion against Velázquez, Cortés convinced the Spaniards to send all of the treasure they had previously received from the Aztecs

Cortés kept his discontented followers from abandoning the expedition by destroying his ships, thereby preventing them from returning to nearby islands.

to the Spanish royal family. Cortés appointed Puertocarrero to oversee this mission, and from then on Malinche rode with Cortés.

Meanwhile, he moved the Spaniards to a new site, twenty-five miles away, where the first buildings of the new town were constructed. Then Cortés took a drastic step: Realizing that his plan to go from the coast to the cities of the Aztecs, a place in the high mountains, would never be accepted by Velázquez's supporters, he ordered that the expedition's ships be stripped of anything useful and then destroyed. His decision forced the Spaniards to be marooned in a strange land, hundreds of miles from help, and surrounded by hostile warriors. "Now we must conquer or die," Cortés is said to have told his men.

Soon after, some natives from a nearby town came to Cortés. They were Totonacs, a native Indian people who lived in a group of some fifty cities that had been previously conquered by the Aztecs. They were cruelly oppressed with heavy taxes and other demands from the Aztecs, including the request for sacrificial victims, a common religious practice of the Aztec people. Cortés agreed to help the Totonacs against the Aztecs, and marched his men to Cempoala, the capital of the Totonac region.

After he arrived at the capital and pledged to help the Totonacs, he requested their total allegiance to the king of Spain and to Christianity. Soon after, five tax collectors from the Aztec Empire also arrived. Cortés convinced the Totonacs to imprison them, though he prevented their sacrifice. His actions resulted in a revolt against the Aztecs and forced the Totonacs to become his allies. But Cortés did not stop there; he secretly allowed two of the tax collectors to escape, sending them to the capital to tell their emperor that Cortés was not really the cause of the revolt, but merely wanted to meet him.

Cortés then told the Totonacs that they must get rid of their idols. They first resisted his request, but Cortés insisted, telling them that the Christian god would protect them now. He and his men destroyed the idols in the temple and erected a cross in their place.

Cortés now prepared to march to the Aztec city of Tenochtitlán. The Totonacs offered him their army, but he took only a thousand men to carry his equipment and pull the cannons. Leaving a hundred Spaniards at Vera Cruz, he set off into the mountains.

# 4

# THE CONQUEST

*And we have always held that those who descended from him would come and conquer this land and take us as their vassals. So because of the place you come from . . . and the things that you tell us about the great lord who sent you . . . we shall obey you and hold you as our lord.*
—Montezuma, emperor of the Aztecs, as reported by Cortés

There were many factors that allowed Cortés to conquer Mexico: his horses, the superior steel weapons and fighting ability of the Spanish, and his own masterful strategy. However, the reaction of the Aztecs and their emperor to Cortés and his army was just as influential to the outcome.

The emperor of the Aztecs, Montezuma—called Moctezuma by the Aztecs—was a man in his fifties, and the ninth emperor of the Aztec, or Mexica, people. The Mexica, named as such after their own conquest of the Mexican region, were not native to the area they occupied when Cortés arrived, but had migrated south over a period of many years. Fierce warriors, the Aztecs had conquered all the peoples of what is now

central Mexico and had built a magnificent capital city, Tenochtitlán, on an island in the middle of a lake in the Valley of Mexico.

## Montezuma and the Aztecs

Montezuma had been a warrior and general, but he was also a priest who was in charge of all the rituals of the Aztec religion, which were central to their entire society.

The chief god of the Aztecs was known as Huitzilopochtli, which literally means "left-handed hummingbird." According to the Aztecs, this god had many forms, including the god of war. They believed that the gods controlled everything in the universe such as the rising and setting of the sun and the success or failure of crops.

The Aztecs also believed that, in order for their gods to remain pleased, they needed to be fed every day. They firmly believed that the gods would become angry or even die if they were not fed. The trouble was that the only food that the Aztecs believed was worthy of feeding the gods was the human heart. Therefore, the Aztecs practiced human sacrifice on a massive scale.

Montezuma, as seen in this sixteenth-century illustration, was the ninth Aztec emperor of Mexico. In 1502, he succeeded his uncle Ahuitzotl as the leader of an empire that had, at the time, reached its greatest extent, stretching from Mexico to the borders of Guatemala. Although Montezuma was commander of the army and organized extensive expeditions of conquest, he was profoundly influenced by his belief in the god Huitzilopochtli, which caused widespread discontent among the Aztec people due to Montezuma's constant requests for human victims to sacrifice.

Aztec priests took sacrificial victims to the top of the pyramidlike temples. The priests would then stretch them out on an altar. While several men held a victim's limbs, the main priest would then take a stone knife and remove his still-beating heart out of his chest. Then his body would be thrown down the stone steps to the pyramid's bottom. Once there, his legs, arms, and head would be removed for various purposes. In some cases, the legs and arms were cooked and eaten.

Human and animal sacrifices were an integral part of the Aztec religion. As they saw it, the continual offering of blood through sacrifice ensured the perpetuation of the universe. They sacrificed 10,000 to 50,000 people each year, the majority of whom were war captives. But common adults and children were also sacrificed. Cortés himself was disgusted at the thought of human sacrifice. This enabled him to gain respect and allies among the Mexican tribes that opposed the Aztecs.

Whenever possible, the Aztecs avoided sacrificing their own people. Instead, captives were killed, sometimes after an elaborate ritual called the War of the Flowers, where instead of trying to kill their enemies they captured them alive to serve as human sacrifices.

The Aztecs had many other gods. The second most important was Quetzalcóatl, which translates in Nahuatl to "feathered serpent." According to legend, he was a bearded man with pale skin who had lived

The god Quetzalcóatl was the Aztec patron of priests, the inventor of the calendar and of books, the protector of craftsmen, and the symbol of death and resurrection.

among the Toltecs, whose heirs the Aztecs claimed to be, as the king of the city of Tula. Quetzalcóatl hated human sacrifice, which put him at odds with the other gods. While the Aztec legend claimed that he had been forced to leave for a country across the ocean in the east, he promised one day to return.

# An Aztec Prophecy

When news of a strange, pale-skinned, bearded man who had come across the water with many seemingly magical weapons and animals reached Montezuma, he was troubled. He questioned his advisors. Was this Quetzalcóatl, returning to seek his vengeance on the gods who had exiled him? According to Aztec prophecy, this would mean the end of the empire. Because he was not certain if Cortés was a god or not, Montezuma hesitated, refusing to send his army to crush him while it was still possible. It was in this way that the road for the conquest of the Aztec Empire was opened.

Cortés and his men marched through the coastal jungles and into the mountains of central Mexico. The air grew cooler as they ascended, and snow was visible on the mountain peaks. They came upon the Aztec city of Xocotla, where they were treated rudely. The Aztecs of the city said that they should head for the important religious center of Cholula, but the Totonac guides traveling with Cortés said that he should instead head for Tlaxcala, an independent kingdom that had long fought against the Aztecs. Cortés took their advice, hoping to again reinforce his army, and marched for Tlaxcala.

Along the way, they were attacked several times by the Tlaxcalans, who feared these strangers as much as they feared the Aztecs. The battles were fierce, with as many as 40,000 Indians attacking the Spaniards, who were less than 400 men. Still, the Spanish cavalry and cannons proved to be too much for the Tlaxcalans, who were easily defeated. They then invited Cortés and his men to come into their city.

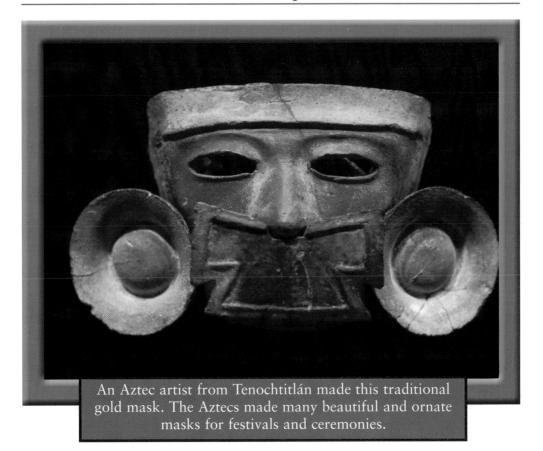

An Aztec artist from Tenochtitlán made this traditional gold mask. The Aztecs made many beautiful and ornate masks for festivals and ceremonies.

Cortés, who wrote several letters to King Charles described the religious city, saying that it was "much larger than Granada [one of the most important cities in Spain], and very much stronger, with as good buildings and many more people." While Cortés was in Tlaxcala, Montezuma again sent him gold and treasure, and promised to give the Spanish king tribute (taxes) in slaves and gold every year. But he also ordered Cortés to leave and not continue on his path to Tenochtitlán.

Cortés again politely refused. He wanted to meet Montezuma face to face. And he felt stronger and more powerful than ever before, for Cortés was now beginning to make powerful allies. In addition to the Totonacs, who were rebelling against the Aztecs, he had also subdued the Tlaxcalans, who had never been defeated by the Aztecs and who were now siding with the Spanish. The Tlaxcalans assembled an army of some 100,000 men and began to follow Cortés to the Aztec capital.

## Advance to Cholula

Next, Cortés advanced to the region of Cholula, an important city which housed a massive temple dedicated to the god Quetzalcóatl. At first, the Cholulans treated the Spanish kindly, bringing them food and allowing them to sleep in their palaces. After several days, however, their attitudes changed. On the flat roofs of their houses, piles of stones appeared, obviously ready to be thrown down upon the invaders. Malinche came to Cortés and told him that the Cholulans were getting ready to attack, and he responded with a shocking act of violence.

The next morning, thousands of Cholulans arrived in the courtyard of the palace where the Spaniards dozed. Although it was later claimed that many of Cortés's men

The Aztecs, who were gripped by the constant belief that natural events had supernatural significance, believed that the eruption of the volcano Popocatépetl *(above)*, was an omen of bad times to come. Located in central Mexico, Popocatépetl lies along Mexico's volcanic axis at the southern edge of the Mexican Plateau, ten miles from another volcano, Iztaccihuatl.

were armed, historians do not know if this is true. What is known is that Cortés had the courtyard sealed, and then led his men in a bloody massacre of the trapped Cholulans. His Tlaxcalan allies, whom he had ordered to remain outside the city, heard the cannon and musket fire, and attacked the town themselves, looting and burning everything in their path. Approximately 3,000 Cholulans died that day, a bloody indication of the fate of anyone who attempted to resist the Spanish takeover.

The Spanish remained in Cholula for a short time before heading to the Valley of Mexico. They passed the huge volcano Popocatépetl, which was erupting—an event the Aztecs took as an omen of bad times to come. Then, from the mountain heights, they beheld the beautiful Valley of Mexico. Far below them, around the large, marshy Lake Texcoco, were many cities of stone, magnificent even from this great distance. There was a large island in the lake, connected to the shore by causeways that crossed the shallow regions of the water. Tenochtitlán was the largest and most beautiful of the Aztec cities, glittering white in the sunlight.

As they began to descend into the valley, an emissary from Montezuma again met them. It was the emperor's nephew, Cacama, and he had a message. He urged the Spanish to leave the region. Cortés, never wavering, refused once more, saying he must meet Montezuma.

On November 8, 1519, a righteous and confident Cortés led his men to Tenochtitlán. The causeway was wide enough for four horsemen, but there were frequent gaps in the path, bridged

Cortés's Indian allies, such as the Tlaxcalans and the Totonacs *(left)*, were vital in helping him defeat the Aztecs; in fact, without other Indians, he would have had no chance against the Aztec Empire. Cortés was able to gain valuable Indian allies through his anti-Aztec policies. To many Indians, who comprised a large percentage of Cortés's forces, the Spanish represented their only hope of breaking the Aztec's cruel suppression. They gave Cortés valuable information about Tenochtitlán, telling him about the number of drawbridges on the causeways, and even the depth of the water in the lake.

over with wooden boards that could be removed to allow canoes to sail through—or to cut off the capital from the shore. Crossbowmen and musketeers followed the horsemen, many clad in quilted cotton armor, sufficient to stop arrows or stones. In a procession behind them came the Tlaxcalan army.

At a fortress on the way, Montezuma and his court met Cortés and his soldiers. The emperor approached the conquistador on shoes of gold. Cortés tried to embrace him, but was prevented from touching his sacred body. Finally, Montezuma invited Cortés to enter the spectacular city.

# Trapped in Tenochtitlán

Cortés's months of planning and manipulation had at last allowed him an entrance to the capital of the Aztec Empire without a battle. Montezuma gave Cortés and his men his father's palace as their quarters, as well as many servants and gifts of gold.

The Spanish marveled at the wealth of Tenochtitlán. The great market of Tlatelolco was larger than any in Spain, and sold strange imported goods, foods, and spices from every corner of the empire. The houses were well built, and the city, cleaner than those in Europe, was crisscrossed with many canals that served to transport goods to and from the capital. Cortés also noticed the lovely

Cortés's house in Mexico, seen here, was built by Indian labor and was overseen by a Spaniard.

hanging gardens of the city and remarked about their unusual beauty.

He asked Montezuma to take him to the top of the huge pyramid that was the Aztecs' main religious temple. Once there he examined their idols, which were literally covered in human blood. Cortés asked if he might erect a Christian cross and a shrine to the Virgin Mary inside the temples so Montezuma could then see which god was most powerful. But the emperor simply refused. He threw the Spaniards out, staying behind to make a sacrifice to the gods to apologize for Cortés's insult.

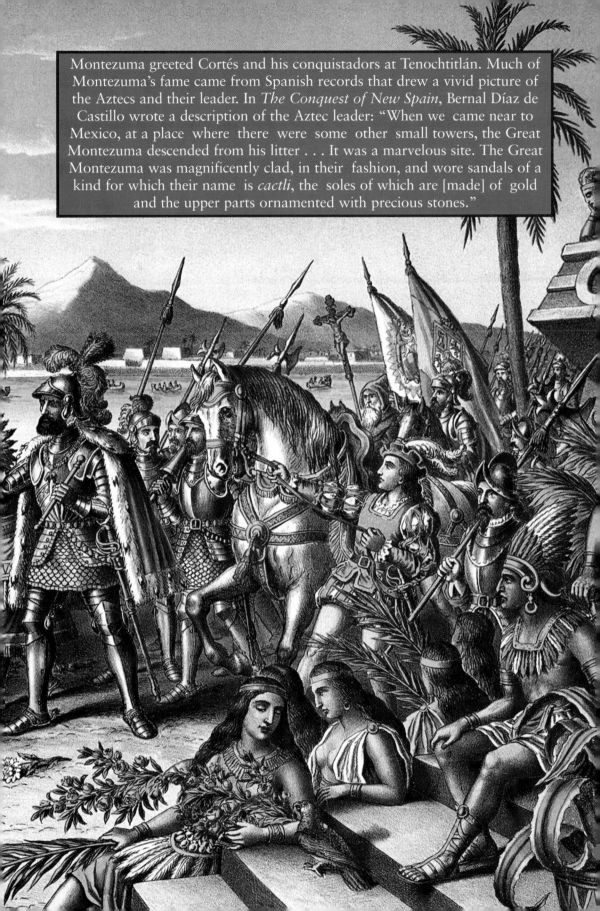

Montezuma greeted Cortés and his conquistadors at Tenochtitlán. Much of Montezuma's fame came from Spanish records that drew a vivid picture of the Aztecs and their leader. In *The Conquest of New Spain*, Bernal Díaz de Castillo wrote a description of the Aztec leader: "When we came near to Mexico, at a place where there were some other small towers, the Great Montezuma descended from his litter . . . It was a marvelous site. The Great Montezuma was magnificently clad, in their fashion, and wore sandals of a kind for which their name is *cactli*, the soles of which are [made] of gold and the upper parts ornamented with precious stones."

Cortés was constantly troubled by the danger his men were in. He knew they were trapped inside Tenochtitlán, now without any ships to escape. The Spaniards were relying on the Aztecs for their food, and could easily be attacked at any time. With his usual boldness, Cortés devised a plan that was both shocking and laughable: Cortés wanted take Montezuma as his hostage.

Cortés went to the emperor with four of his most trusted men, including Bernal Díaz del Castillo, and requested that the Aztec leader come to stay at Montezuma's father's palace. Montezuma was outraged, but realizing that Cortés's men were ready to kill him immediately, Montezuma offered instead to give Cortés one of his sons as a hostage.

Cortés dismissed the idea. Surely, he said, there would be nothing wrong with the emperor staying in the house of his own father, close by his foreign guests. Montezuma, astonishingly, agreed to come. Perhaps he felt that fate was closing in on him, and that Cortés really had come to punish the Aztec people. Or maybe he had simply given up. At any rate, from that moment forward, Montezuma was a Spanish prisoner.

# The Great Hostage

The Spanish stayed in Tenochtitlán for more than eight months, most of those in luxury. They built three sailing ships, which

Knowing that the Aztecs would not attack as long as he held Montezuma captive, Cortés trapped the great Aztec leader while his men seized Aztec wealth by force and in Montezuma's name.

the Aztecs had never seen before, and took Montezuma on cruises across the lake. The Spanish grew very fond of the emperor, who was intelligent and generous, frequently giving the Spanish gifts of gold, jewels, and slaves. The amount of treasure taken by the Spanish was staggering, including an enormous hoard of gold and silver that they had found in a hidden room while living in the palace.

Cortés, by holding Montezuma captive, had practically become the ruler of the Aztec Empire already, although he issued all of

Cortés supervised the building of his ships by Aztec slaves for his escape from Mexico, but later admitted that his intention was only to create a diversion, as well as an effort to bide his time in Tenochtitlán.

his commands in Montezuma's name. He even struck sacred Aztec idols with an iron bar, enraging the priests. Cortés also took Indian rebels from the coast and burned them at the stake in Tenochtitlán's main square. These incidents seem to have roused the imprisoned emperor. By April 1520, Montezuma told Cortés that the Aztecs were turning against him. They were angry that he had taken away their gods. He recommended that Cortés and his men leave. Cortés replied that he must build new ships. To accomplish this he sent a large group of Indian slaves to the coast with some of his men to begin building them, although later Cortés claimed that his intentions were false: He had no plan of completing such a project. Meanwhile, he had sent small parties of Spaniards to every corner of the empire, always searching for golden treasure and profitable luxuries. Then a crisis arose that Cortés did not expect.

His lieutenant, Puertocarrero, who had been sent in a ship to deliver the Spanish gold directly to King Charles, did not obey his orders and instead stopped in Cuba along the way. It was because of this detour that Diego Velázquez heard about Cortés's attempt to claim all of Mexico for himself. He assembled an expedition of 900 men, under the command of Panfílo de Narváez, to find Cortés and arrest him. They landed at Vera Cruz in April of 1520 and soon began to advance into the mountains.

When Cortés first heard about this new expedition he was pleased, thinking that the soldiers had come as reinforcements for his tired army. But when Narváez sent men to demand the surrender of Vera Cruz, Cortés discovered his true intentions. The timing could hardly have been worse for Cortés, since his forces were completely scattered. Leaving Pedro de Alvarado in command of the remaining Spanish in Tenochtitlán, he set out with seventy men to intercept Narváez. Along the way he was joined by more of

This Aztec drawing shows Cortés's conquistadors and the Tlaxcalans fighting with other Native Americans.

his soldiers, but his force was still small. As the 250 men approached Cempoala, the capital of the Totonac kingdom, Narváez and his men established a camp.

## Spaniards Against Spaniards

Waiting until nightfall, Cortés surrounded the other Spaniards, who were gathered around the temple of Cempoala, and attacked suddenly. Narváez's men were surprised; many who were not particularly loyal to Narváez surrendered immediately. Narváez was stabbed in one eye and taken prisoner. As soon as he met Cortés, he congratulated the conquistador for capturing him. "The least deed I have done in this land is capture you," Cortés replied.

Many of Narváez's men, seeing the gold jewelry worn by Cortés's army, switched sides. This increased Cortés's force to some 1,100 men, including more than 100 on horseback. He also had the assistance of 8,000 Tlaxcalan warriors, and soon it became apparent that he would need each one of them. Cortés quickly marched his army back to the capital, for there was trouble brewing in Tenochtitlán.

Alone in a hostile land, Alvarado had panicked. Believing that the Aztecs were getting ready to assault him, he ordered his men to attack during an important religious ceremony. Thousands of people were packed into one of the great squares of Tenochtitlán. Hundreds or thousands of Aztecs were killed in a bloody replay of the massacre at Cholula. Enraged, the Aztec warriors had risen and forced the Spanish to take refuge in their palace.

# A Night of Sorrow

The Aztecs allowed Cortés and his large army to march directly inside the palace, but it was a trap: They wanted only to pack the entire army inside the palace and secure its exits. It had been almost two weeks

since the Spanish had been last attacked, but those who had remained in Tenochtitlán were anxious. They had little food or water. The following day, the Aztecs struck.

Days went by and they fought without stopping. The Aztecs fired burning arrows into the thatched roof of the palace, causing many fires. Rocks, arrows, and spears rained down on the Spanish defenders. Several times Cortés sent his cavalry out of the palace, attempting to force their way out, but each time they were driven back. Since brute force failed, Cortés again turned to diplomacy and sent Montezuma to the palace walls to order his people to stop fighting, but it was too late. The Aztecs would no longer listen to their emperor. Stones and arrows were thrown at him, crushing his head. With no desire to live, Montezuma lingered on for three days before dying, all the while refusing to convert to Christianity.

Cortés knew that the Spanish had to escape from the city. He had the huge hoard of treasure they had taken melted down and distributed to his men, although he warned them not to carry so much that they would not be able to move quickly. On the night of June 30, 1520, the Spanish and

This dramatic nineteenth-century image shows Montezuma's death. Montezuma's submission to the Spaniards had eroded the respect of his people. According to Spanish accounts, he attempted to speak to his subjects and was assailed with stones and arrows, suffering wounds from which he died three days later. The Aztecs believed the Spaniards had murdered their emperor, and Cortés's forces were nearly destroyed as they tried to sneak out of Tenochtitlán at night.

Realizing the hopelessness of the situation, Cortés attempted to retreat on the night of June 30, 1520 (commonly referred to in Mexico today as *La Noche Triste*, or "the Sad Night"). While he was crossing the bridge leaving the city of Tenochtitlán, the Aztecs fell upon the army and inflicted them with many wounds. During the battle, some Spanish soldiers who had greedily filled their pockets with too much gold were pushed into Lake Texcoco where they drowned.

their remaining Indian allies began to creep out of the palace. They attempted to travel along the causeway heading to the shore. They were soon discovered, however, and were fiercely attacked. A canoe full of warriors came alongside the Spaniards, firing arrows and stones at them.

Through the shower of piercing arrows, hundreds of Spaniards tried to escape. Cortés and his men demonstrated enormous courage and paid a high price: More than 800 Spaniards died that night, leaving merely

400 to escape. They had lost all of their muskets and cannons, but they were alive. Cortés, though seriously wounded, had not given up his quest to conquer the Aztec people.

The Spanish conquistadors began to march toward Tlaxcala. Along the way they were attacked by a large army of Aztecs and nearly destroyed. During the battle, however, the Spaniards managed to kill the Aztec army's main general, a result that intimidated even the strongest of the Aztec fighters. After the battle ceased, the Spaniards limped into Tlaxcala.

# Return to the Valley of Mexico

Despite their miserable condition, Cortés's men remained loyal to him. Within several weeks, he had recovered enough to take action again, helping the Tlaxcalans conquer the neighboring land of Tepeaca, a province of the Aztec Empire that lay on the best route from Vera Cruz to Tenochtitlán. Slowly, reinforcements from Spain and the colonies arrived, bringing horses, muskets, and cannons. Cortés began planning his return to the Valley of Mexico.

Since the Aztecs had thousands of warriors capable of surrounding their city in canoes, they could attack anyone on the causeways trying to enter Tenochtitlán. Realizing that he must find a way to prevent this if he

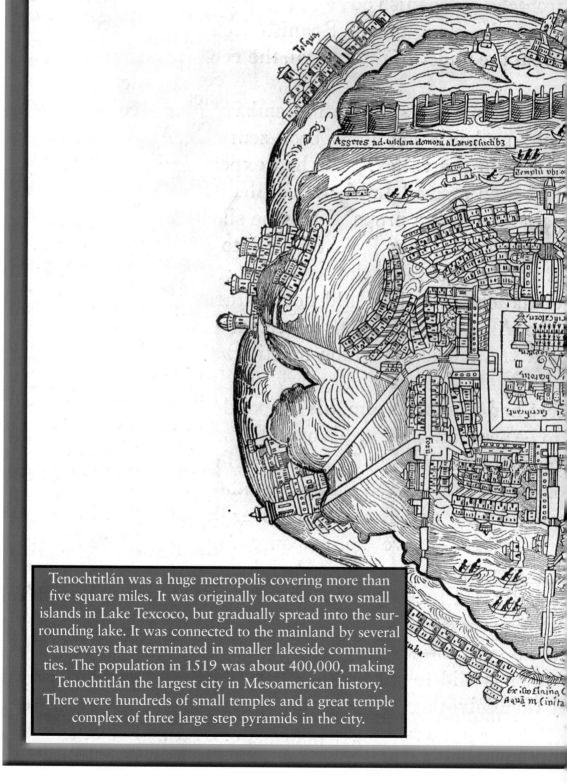

Tenochtitlán was a huge metropolis covering more than five square miles. It was originally located on two small islands in Lake Texcoco, but gradually spread into the surrounding lake. It was connected to the mainland by several causeways that terminated in smaller lakeside communities. The population in 1519 was about 400,000, making Tenochtitlán the largest city in Mesoamerican history. There were hundreds of small temples and a great temple complex of three large step pyramids in the city.

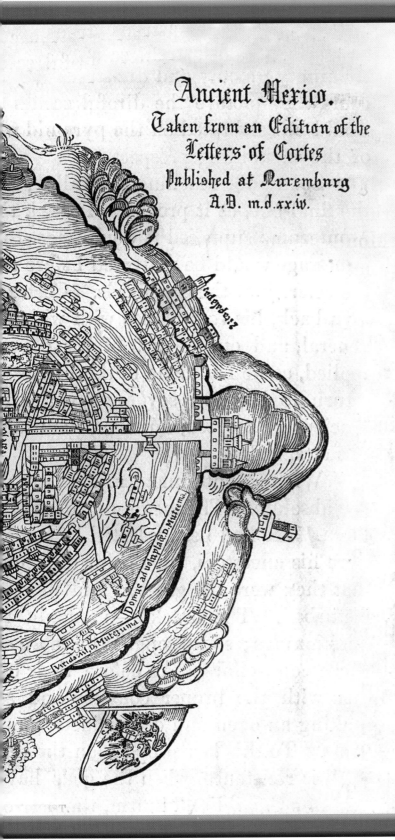

Ancient Mexico.
Taken from an Edition of the
Letters of Cortes
Published at Nuremburg
A.D. m.d.xx.iv.

hoped to capture the city, Cortés ordered the construction of thirteen sailing ships. These were built on the dry land of Tlaxcala, and then disassembled and carried by thousands of Indians to the Valley of Mexico.

Cortés had another weapon he wasn't even aware of: smallpox, an invisible killer that was destroying the Aztec Empire from the inside. This terrible, disfiguring disease had plagued Europe for thousands of years, but was unknown in the Americas. Many of Cortés's men had already been exposed to the disease and were immune, but the native people had no such resistance and quickly died by the thousands.

Cortés's plan was to capture the cities around Lake Texcoco and then move on the capital itself. His first target was Texcoco, a city he captured with an army of forty men on horseback and more than 550 foot soldiers, along with thousands of Indian allies. When Cortés and his men approached the city on January 1, 1521, its king fled. Cortés appointed a new king and the entire city sided with him. Because many of the Aztec cities were unhappy with Mexican rule, Cortés used their discontent to his advantage.

While the Texcocans reassembled his ships, Cortés attacked several other cities around the lake and finally captured Chapultepec, the source of fresh water for Tenochtitlán. (Most of Lake Texcoco was salty and not fit for drinking.)

By May of 1521, Cortés was ready to launch the attack on Tenochtitlán. Reinforcements had continued to arrive, and he now had nearly a thousand men with him, including almost a hundred men on horseback and perhaps as many as 200,000 Indian allies. Each of his thirteen ships was fitted with a cannon that had been brought by Spanish reinforcements. These ships, called brigantines by Cortés, had both sails and oars. Each carried about twenty men, along with several crossbows and muskets.

On June 1, 1521, Cortés launched his small fleet. The Aztec canoes were no match for his ships—they plowed right through them—and the Spaniards used spears and muskets to kill the Aztecs who were thrown into the water. The sails made the ships faster than any canoe, and their cannons were used to attack warriors on the causeways.

By June 9, Cortés and his men reached Tenochtitlán and the attack began. Using the brigantines to keep the Aztecs from attacking from the water, the Spanish marched over three different causeways and were soon fighting inside the city itself, beginning a month of bloody conflict. Each day the Spanish would assault the Aztecs, driving them farther and farther inside the city, but the Aztecs stubbornly fought back. By now, however, their food and water supplies were depleted, and disease further weakened them.

Even though the Aztecs had some 1,500 canoes, they were no match for the small fleet of brigantine ships built by Cortés's army. Shortly after their launch, Cortés ordered that each ship bombard the lake, immediately destroying dozens of Aztec canoes, while the Aztec attempted to swim to safety. Soon Cortés surrounded Tenochtitlán. By controlling the lake, Cortés was able to block any escape routes and prevent food and supplies from reaching the city.

A massive assault by the Spanish on June 30 cost them greatly. They watched in horror as the Aztecs sacrificed some fifty Spanish prisoners they had taken, rolling their mutilated corpses down the long staircase of the great temple.

Afterward, Cortés decided that he must destroy the beautiful city, since he would never be able to capture it with so many of its buildings still standing as ready-made fortresses for the Aztec defenders. His men continued to advance, destroying everything in their path and pushing the remaining Aztecs to the very edge of their beloved lake. Their new emperor, Cuauhtemoc, who had led them bravely, was finally captured by one of Cortés's brigantines as he tried to flee. Finally, with his capture, the Aztecs surrendered. On August 13, 1521, one of the greatest empires in the history of the Americas ceased to exist.

# 5

# THE CONQUEROR

*He bore himself nobly, with such gravity and prudence that he never gave offence or seemed unapproachable . . . He was devout and given to praying; he knew many prayers and psalms by heart . . . he ordinarily gave a thousand ducats a year to charity, and sometimes lent money for alms, saying that with the interest he would expiate his sins . . . Such, just as you have heard, was Cortés, Conqueror of New Spain.*
—Francisco López de Gómara, *History of the Conquest of Mexico*

With the fall of Tenochtitlán, most resistance to the Spanish invasion ended. But Cortés's tasks were far from over, for, having dealt with two Mexican emperors, he now had to deal with a Spanish one.

The conquistadors succeeded where generations of Aztec rulers had failed. A major influence on the Spanish conquest of Mexico was the dissension among the different native groups in the Aztec Empire. The Aztec overlords made no attempt to integrate these other native cultures into their own. This provided the basis for a full-scale revolt against them, which Cortés incited. While the Aztecs were unable to unify the Aztec Empire, the Spaniards succeeded. With diligent work by missionaries and Cortés himself, the Spaniards united the people of Mexico and the southwestern United States by converting them to Christianity. The resulting extension of Spanish territories, called New Spain, was strongly united for years afterward.

While Cortés's accomplishments were clearly among the greatest military feats in history, there remained the question as to whether or not they were legal under Spanish law. This was important not because the Spanish would give the Aztecs back their empire if Cortés's actions were illegal, but because Cortés would lose his claim to the vast lands he had acquired for Spain if he had exceeded his authority. As he expected, he would certainly lose his share of Aztec treasure.

Cortés knew that he had been disloyal to Diego Velázquez by ignoring his orders, founding his own town, and marching into the interior of Mexico. Still, he had sent an appeal to King Charles. If the king supported him, then Cortés would be safe from any legal problems.

Getting to speak to the king was particularly difficult, however. Charles was not only king of Spain; he was the ruler of a vast region of Germany and central Europe. Because of his responsibilities to the empire, he spent very little time in Spain. Velázquez also had powerful allies in Spain, most notably Bishop Fonseca, the head of the council of the Indies and practically the ruler of all of Spain's colonies. He had seized the treasure that Cortés had sent back to Spain and brought serious accusations against him.

# Governor of New Spain

Cortés had troubles of his own in Mexico. He was building its new capital on the ruins of Tenochtitlán while his men continued to explore and add land to his holdings. He also began to grant estates to his followers, recreating the hated encomienda system in New Spain even though a royal decree had tried to end the practice. This defiance would later cause trouble for Cortés. (Although he had been opposed to the encomienda system while on the island of Hispaniola, Cortés found that it would be impossible to maintain control of his men without giving them grants of land. As was usual for Cortés, he was certain to keep the best plots for himself.)

Thanks to the efforts of his father back home and other noblemen, Cortés was backed by the king and named governor of New Spain in 1523. But his life continued to be blemished by controversy. One of his rivals, Francisco de Garay, the governor of Jamaica, tried to found his own colony in Mexico. Cortés sent his men to establish a town in the region Garay wished to settle. Once he was confirmed as governor of New Spain, Cortés invited Garay to come to Mexico City, where the two men resolved their differences. But because Garay died soon after, rumors began spreading that Cortés had poisoned him.

**MEXICO**

←1519 route

◄··Retreat, 1520

←1521 route

▭ Aztec Empire

• Town or City

▲ Volcano

Tenochtitlán •

*PACIFIC*
*OCEAN*

N

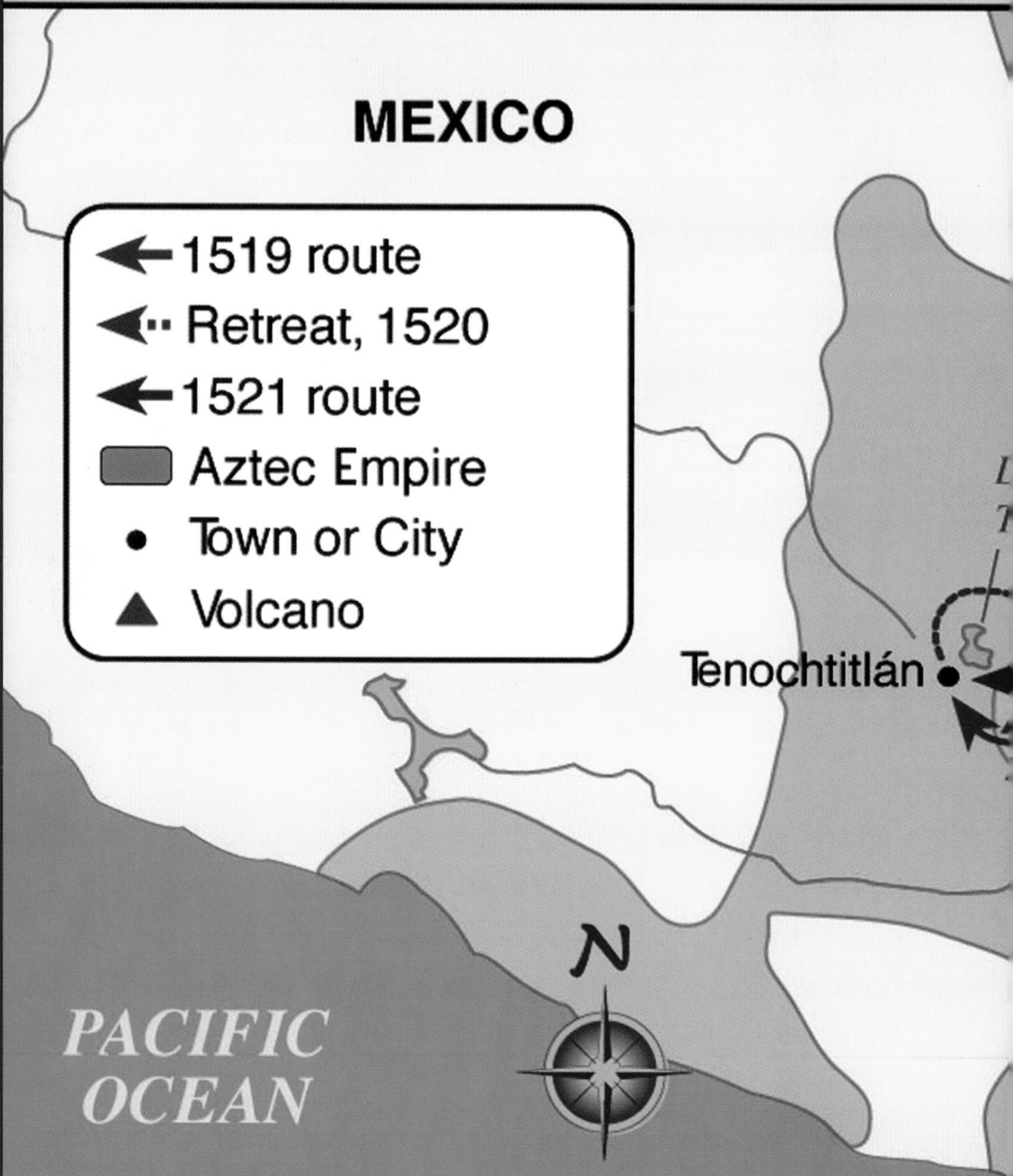

This map shows Cortés's routes of conquest into the Aztec Empire.

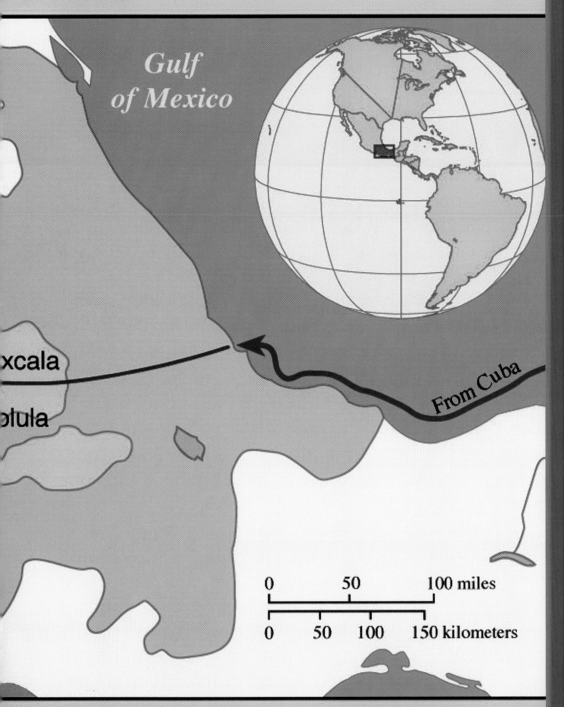

# Cortés

Gulf
of Mexico

xcala

olula

From Cuba

0      50      100 miles

0    50    100    150 kilometers

# Suspicions Mount

This was not the only suspicious death that happened near Cortés. His wife, Catalina, unexpectedly visited him in the summer of 1522. Cortés and Catalina were no longer close and he had fathered several children with native women, including Malinche. But he welcomed Catalina with a huge banquet and feast. Within three months, she was dead—supposedly from asthma (the thin mountain air of Mexico City was unhealthy for people with that disease). Nonetheless many Spaniards were suspicious about her untimely death.

In 1524, Cortés organized an expedition to explore the region now known as Honduras. He chose as the leader of the expedition one of his most loyal lieutenants, Cristóbal de Olid. But Olid, having talked to Velázquez in Cuba, decided to take Cortés's lead. He established his own settlement in Honduras and declared himself an independent conquistador, just as Cortés had done earlier at Vera Cruz.

Cortés sent a strong force by sea to attack Olid. Then he took another army south himself, crossing the dense jungles of Honduras. It was the worst decision of his career. He spent several months cutting his way through hostile rain forest, finally stumbling into a Spanish settlement in Honduras. Aged greatly by his journey, Cortés found that the men he sent to sea had killed Olid.

Then news came that the men he had left in charge in Mexico City, agents of the king sent to help him run the country, had turned against him. Cortés hurried back by sea to Vera Cruz, where he was nearly unrecognizable, so much had he suffered in Honduras. He was able to restore order in the capital, but now he was in even more trouble with the rulers of Spain.

After hearing the many different charges made against Cortés by his enemies, the king decided to conduct a *residencia*, or an investigation, into how he was ruling Mexico. For the next several years Cortés was suspended from the post of governor of New Spain. Cortés warmly welcomed the lawyer sent to conduct the investigation, Luis Ponce de León, but a few days later the official was dead, apparently of a disease that had also killed a man on the ship that brought him to Mexico. His successor, Marcos de Aguilar, an elderly man with a bad stomach, died seven months later. Once again suspicion about the death fell on Cortés.

## A Final Return

Cortés decided to return to Spain in order to tell his story to the king. In 1528, he loaded a massive treasure of gold, as well as many strange animals and several Aztec slaves, onto two ships and sailed back to Spain, arriving in Palos in April of that year. It was his first return in twenty-four years.

In the autumn of that year he met King Charles for the first time. Impressed by Cortés's loyalty and clearheaded thinking concerning the administration of Spain's new empire, the king rewarded him richly, naming him the marquis of the valley of Oaxaca, a fertile valley that stretched across central Mexico. Cortés was now lord of an area about one-fourth the size of Spain itself. But King Charles refused to restore Cortés to the governorship of New Spain.

Cortés stayed in Spain until 1530, marrying again, this time a beautiful noblewoman, Doña Juana de Zúñiga. Their marriage was happy and they had a son, Don Martín, and three daughters.

While Cortés had been in Spain, a council called an *audiencia* had been established to rule New Spain in his absence. The first audiencia was composed of his enemies, who refused to allow Cortés to enter Mexico City. As a result, he stayed in Texcoco until a second audiencia arrived from Spain. But his days as ruler of Mexico were over.

Cortés retired to the western coast of Mexico. He sent several expeditions into the Pacific, searching for new lands to add to the Spanish Empire, as well as the fabled water passage that would allow ships from Spain to sail directly to the East Indies. (This passage did not exist until the construction of the Panama Canal in the twentieth century.) Unfortunately, his expeditions failed to find anything of interest, although he did sail to Baja California, giving his name to the Sea of Cortés between that peninsula and the mainland of Mexico.

Cortés had sunk a fortune into these explorations and gotten little out of them. A life of inactivity, however, was intolerable. The new viceroy of Mexico refused to allow him to send out expeditions to the new lands the Spanish were conquering in North and South America. Once again, Cortés decided to return to Spain and plead his case to King Charles.

He arrived in there in 1540, but soon found that his influence had vanished. The king had bigger problems than helping out the marquis of the valley; the Protestant Reformation was causing a civil war in Germany, and the crushing taxes King Charles had put on Spain to pay off his debts were causing widespread discontent among the citizens. In 1541, Cortés accompanied King Charles in an attack against one of the rulers of Algeria, but a massive storm wrecked the Spanish fleet and the attack failed before it could begin. Cortés offered to stay behind and attack the Algerians anyway, but he was laughed at instead.

Cortés returned to Spain, where he lingered for six years, out of favor and unable to see the king. He decided to return to Mexico, but the greatest of all the conquistadors died on December 2, 1547, before he could set sail.

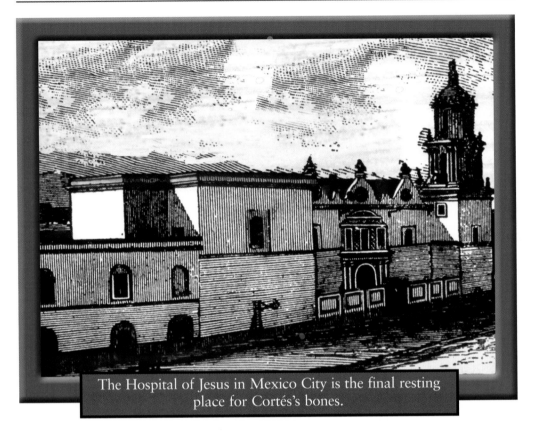

The Hospital of Jesus in Mexico City is the final resting place for Cortés's bones.

In 1566, Cortés's bones were taken from Spain to Texcoco, in Mexico. They were later moved again and reburied several times before coming to rest in the Hospital of Jesus in Mexico City, which Cortés had founded. During the Mexican War of Independence in 1823, in fear that revolutionaries would destroy the bones, they were hidden within a wall in an abandoned church. There they lay for more than a hundred years until archaeologists uncovered them. They remain there still, a symbol of Mexico's past, and as controversial today as the great captain was in his own time.

# CHRONOLOGY

**1485**  Hernán Cortés is born in Medellín, Extremadura.

**1492**  The last of Moorish Spain is reconquered by the Spanish.

**1499**  Cortés, some believe, is sent to the University of Salamanca to study law.

**1502**  Cortés decides to sail to Hispaniola with Nicolás de Ovando, but is injured before the journey.

**1504**  Cortés finally leaves Spain for Hispaniola under the command of Alonso Quintero. He is granted land and Indian slaves by the governor and is appointed notary of Azúa.

**1511**  Cortés takes part in the Diego Velázquez conquest of Cuba.

**1513**  Cortés is engaged to Catalina Xuárez, and marries her in 1515.

**1517**  Velázquez authorizes an expedition with more than 100 men to explore Central America.

**1518**  Cortés leads an expedition to the Yucatán Peninsula.

**1519**  Cortés is appointed captain-general of the Spanish Armada, lands in San Juan de Ulua, and first meets representatives from the Aztec Empire. He mounts an expedition to conquer the Aztec civilization after securing territory he named Villa Rica de la Vera Cruz, an area he hoped to colonize.

**1521**  The Spanish, with Cortés as their leader, topple the Aztec Empire.

**1521–1650**  The Spanish fully colonize Mexico.

**1522**  Cortés's wife, Catalina, suspiciously dies after visiting her husband.

**1524**  Cortés organizes an expedition to explore the region now known as the Honduras.

**1530**  Cortés remarries, this time to Doña Juana de Zúñiga.

**1547**  Cortés dies in Andalusia, Spain, shortly before he was scheduled to return to Mexico.

# GLOSSARY

**alcalde**  A Spanish word for mayor of a town.

**audiencia**  A council appointed to investigate charges against a Spanish colonial governor.

**Aztec**  The Native American people of central Mexico who conquered and ruled a large empire. Aztec was the original name for these people; after they conquered the Valley of Mexico, they called themselves Mexica.

**brigantine**  A small sailing ship, equipped with oars.

**causeway**  A road that crosses water. Unlike a bridge, which is built above the water, a causeway is actually built up from the bottom of the body of water.

**cavalry**  A group of soldiers mounted on horses.

**conquistador**  A Spanish soldier who explored and conquered regions of the New World.

**Don, Doña**  Spanish words for noble titles; usually translated as "Lord."

**Flower War**  An Aztec custom designed to capture people to be sacrificed to the gods. The warriors who fought in a Flower War did not try to kill their opponents, but capture them alive.

**harquebus**  A primitive firearm carried by the Spanish during the conquest of Mexico. It used a burning piece of cord or fuse called a match to set off the gunpowder. For this reason, this kind of firearm is called a matchlock.

**hidalgo**  A Spanish word meaning "gentleman." A hidalgo was not a noble, but he was higher in status than ordinary people.

**Hispaniola**  A large island in the Caribbean, site of the first Spanish colony in the New World, Santo Domingo. The present-day nations of Haiti and the Dominican Republic are on Hispaniola.

**Huitzilopochtli**   The chief god of the Aztecs; his name meant "hummingbird."

**Iberian Peninsula**   The peninsula of Europe where Spain and Portugal are located.

**infidel**   A person who does not believe in Christianity or Islam; a nonbeliever, usually used by Christians to describe Muslims or Jews.

**Islam**   A religion founded by the prophet Mohammed whose followers worship the god Allah.

**last rites**   A sacrament of the Catholic Church that is given to a person who is in imminent danger of dying.

**marquis**   A title of nobility, usually considered well above a baron or lord, and just below that of a duke.

**Moors**   The Muslim invaders of Spain from North Africa.

**Muslim**   A member of the Islamic religion.

**New World**  The Americas that Columbus
   had "discovered."

**notary public**  An official responsible for certifying
   that documents have been correctly created and
   are legal.

**Quetzalcóatl**  A chief god of the Aztecs, or "feathered
   serpent." Quetzalcóatl was supposed to have once
   taken the form of a pale-skinned man with a beard;
   because of this, the Aztecs may have believed the
   Spanish invaders to be the god or his servants.

**requerimiento**  A document the conquistadors were
   legally bound to read before fighting the natives of
   the Americas. It explained the basics of the Christian
   religion, and told the natives that they must accept
   the rule of the king of Spain.

**residencia**  An official investigation of a Spanish
   colonial governor.

**sanctuary**  A Christian custom which held that a
   person inside a church could not be arrested or
   harmed in any way while he or she remained inside
   the church building.

**stockade**  A high wall of sharpened logs that is used to surround a fort or town.

**stocks**  A method of public punishment. People put in the stocks were locked into a heavy wooden frame by their hands and/or feet, helpless to protect themselves from the ridicule of passersby.

**viceroy**  A person who rules a region in the name of the king.

**Yucatán Peninsula**  A large peninsula of southern Mexico.

# FOR MORE INFORMATION

American Museum of Natural History
Central Park at 79th Street
New York, NY 10024-5192
(212) 769-5606
Web site: http://www.amnh.org/

Natural History Museum of Los Angeles County
900 Exposition Boulevard
Los Angeles, CA 90007
(213) 763-DINO (3466)
Web site: http://www.nhm.org

## Web Sites

Due to the changing nature of Internet links, the Rosen
Publishing Group, Inc., has developed an online list of
Web sites related to the subject of this book. This site
is updated regularly. Please use this link to access
the list:

http://www.rosenlinks.com/lee/heco.html

# FOR FURTHER READING

Barghusen, Joan D. *The Aztecs: End of a Civilization* (History's Great Defeats). San Diego, CA: Lucent Books, 2000.

Crisfield, Deborah, and Patrick O'Brian. *The Travels of Hernán Cortés*. Austin, TX: Raintree Steck-Vaughn, 2000.

De Angelis, Gina. *Hernando Cortés and the Conquest of Mexico* (Explorers of the New World). Broomall, PA: Chelsea House, 2000.

Flowers, Charles. *Cortés and the Conquest of the Aztec Empire in World History*. Berkley Heights, NJ: Enslow Publishers, 2001.

Stein, Conrad R. *The Aztec Empire* (Cultures of the Past). Tarrytown, NY: Marshall Cavendish, 1996.

Tanaka, Shelley. *The Lost Temple of the Aztecs: What It Was Like When the Spaniards Invaded Mexico*. New York: Hyperion Press, 1998.

# BIBLIOGRAPHY

Collis, Maurice. *Cortés and Montezuma*. New York:
New Directions Books, 1954.

Cortés, Hernan. *Letters From Mexico*. Trans. and ed. by
A.R. Pagden. New York: Grossman Publishers, 1971.

de Fuentes, Patricia, ed. and trans. *The Conquistadors*.
New York: Orion Press, 1963.

de Gómara, Francisco López. *Cortés: The Life of the
Conqueror by his Secretary*. Trans. and ed. by Lesley
Byrd Simpson. Los Angeles: University of California
Press, 1965.

Díaz (del Castillo), Bernal. *The Bernal Díaz Chronicles*.
Trans. and ed. by Albert Idell. Garden City, NY:
Doubleday, 1957.

Johnson, William Weber. *Cortés: Conquering the New
World*. New York: Paragon House Publishers, 1987.

Marks, Richard L. *Cortés: The Great Adventurer and
the Fate of Aztec Mexico*. New York: Alfred A.
Knopf, 1993.

Motolinía (Fray Toribio de Benavente). *Motolinía's History of the Indians of New Spain*. Berkeley, CA: University of California Press, 1950.

Portilla, Miguel Léon, ed., and Garibay K., Angel María, trans. *The Broken Spears*. Boston: Beacon, 1962.

Prescott, William Hickling. *History of the Conquest of Mexico*. New York: Harper Bros., 1843.

# INDEX

## About the Author

Fred Ramen is a writer and computer programmer who lives in New York City. His previous titles for the Rosen Publishing Group include biographies of Albert Speer and Joe Montana. Among his interests are military history, science fiction, and French cuisine.

## Photo Credits

Cover, pp. 12, 58 © Archivo Iconografico, S.A./Corbis; pp. 4, 8, 19, 23, 32–33, 37, 40, 44, 46, 60, 69, 74, 76, 89, 98 © North Wind Picture Archives; pp. 11, 54, 70–71, 78 © Bettmann/Corbis; pp. 15, 27 © Corbis; pp. 16–17, 92–93 © maps.com/Corbis; pp. 30, 63 © Charles & Josette Lenars/Corbis; pp. 34, 49, 65, 82–83, 86 © Culver Pictures; p. 52 © Réunion des Musées Nationaux/Art Resource, NY; pp. 61, 73 © Giraudon/Art Resource, NY; pp. 66, 80 © Schalkwijk/Art Resource, NY.

## Series Design

Tahara Hasan

## Layout

Les Kanturek

## Editor

Joann Jovinelly